THE GREAT DEPRESSION
BY THE NUMBERS

BY ANTONIA E. MALCHIK

TABLE OF CONTENTS

Introduction

It was a time when millions of people walked the streets, searching for jobs that did not exist. In 1933, nearly 13 million people in the United States were **unemployed**, or unable to find jobs. They were poor, hungry, and hopeless. This was the Great **Depression**.

Thousands of people stood in line for free bread or a bowl of soup. People crowded around banks, hoping to take out their life savings before the banks closed for good. People walked the city streets, begging for change. The question "Brother, can you spare a dime?" even became the title of a popular song.

During the Great Depression, many families lost their homes. They had to live wherever they could find shelter.

Time Line of the Great Depression

October 29, 1929	Winter 1932–1933	March–June 1933
↓ Black Tuesday; Great Depression starts	↓ Depth of the Great Depression; 13 million unemployed	↓ President Roosevelt creates "New Deal" programs to end the Depression

Franklin D. Roosevelt became president of the United States in 1933. His "New Deal" programs were aimed at giving people jobs and food. You will learn how, despite these programs, millions of families still did not have enough to eat.

The Great Depression was a tragic time in American history. It affected most Americans. As you read, look for the causes of the Great Depression. Learn what life was like for the people who lived through it. Find out how it finally ended. Along the way, you'll solve math problems using numbers related to the Great Depression.

SOLVE THIS!

Labor Force	1930	1933	1940	2000
Employed	45 million	35 million	48 million	137 million
Unemployed	4 million	13 million	8 million	6 million
Unemployment Rate	8%	27%	14%	4%

Use the table above to answer the following questions.

a. The number of people unemployed in 1933 was about three times the number of people unemployed in which year?

b. The unemployment rate increased during which time period? By what percent?

c. How many people were in the labor force in 1940?

une 25, 1938

Congress passes
America's first
minimum-wage law

September 1, 1939

World War II
begins

December 8, 1941

U.S. enters World War II;
Great Depression ends

Causes of the Great Depression

To understand what caused the Great Depression, we must go back to the 1920s.

The Roaring Twenties

The Charleston was a new dance craze. Jazz music played on radio stations across the country. Movie theaters featured silent films with stars like Charlie Chaplin and Mary Pickford. Almost 30 million Model T cars were on the road.

It was the 1920s. World War I was over and America was feeling good.

In the United States, the "Roaring Twenties" were a time of great **prosperity** for many people. Businesses had developed factories and technology that could mass produce goods, and people wanted to buy those goods. In addition to cars, consumers bought washing machines, refrigerators, vacuum cleaners, and other appliances that made their lives easier. Mass production brought new jobs to American cities. For many people, it seemed as if life had never been better.

Women dance the Charleston in 1924.

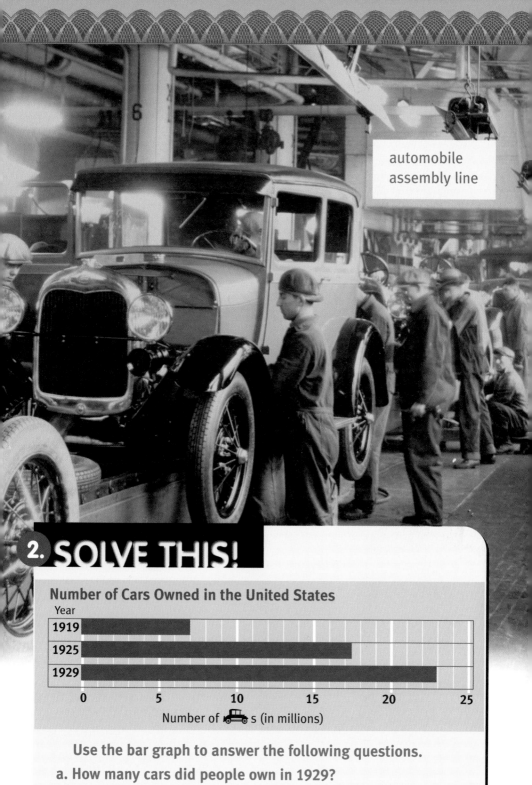

automobile assembly line

SOLVE THIS!

Number of Cars Owned in the United States

Year	
1919	
1925	
1929	

0   5   10   15   20   25

Number of 🚗s (in millions)

Use the bar graph to answer the following questions.

a. How many cars did people own in 1929?

b. How many more cars were owned in 1929 than in 1919?

The "Easy Terms" sign in this store window refers to buying items on credit.

Signs of Trouble to Come

But in the 1920s there were also hints of the trouble to come. For one thing, people were going into debt. Ordinary Americans wanted more and more of the mass-produced goods that brought convenience to their lives. They got these goods by using money they didn't really have. Installment **credit**, paying for things over time, was catching on. A person might buy a $123 radio by paying $1 a week towards its price. People thought they would always have their jobs, so they could pay off their debts in the future.

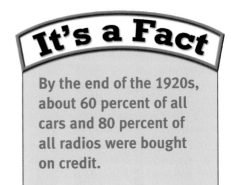

It's a Fact

By the end of the 1920s, about 60 percent of all cars and 80 percent of all radios were bought on credit.

Meanwhile, one group of Americans never experienced the good times of the 1920s. Farmers, far from the booming cities, struggled. During World War I, the government had encouraged them to grow more food crops to sell to countries in Europe. By the 1920s, the war was over and European countries were able to grow enough food on their own. U.S. farmers produced a surplus, or more food than people needed to buy. The farmers had to lower their prices, which meant they earned less money. While many American consumers enjoyed their new electric irons and radios and gas stoves, many farmers could barely feed themselves.

Farmers harvest rye in 1929.

Still, most Americans believed the good times would continue. Business owners, who saw strong sales of their products, produced more and more goods.

Many of these goods could be mail-ordered out of catalogs. Catalog shopping became very popular in the 1920s, especially with people who lived in rural areas, far from stores. People could buy items such as vacuum cleaners and refrigerators, clothing and jewelry, and wagons and plows from catalogs. Some people even bought house-building kits from a catalog!

3. SOLVE THIS!

Use the table called 1920s Salaries to answer the following questions.

a. What was the average weekly salary of a bank clerk?

b. What was the average weekly salary of a farm worker?

1920s Salaries

Job	Average Yearly Salary
Manager	$3,600
Bank clerk	$1,300
Teacher	$900
Office worker (male)	$1,200
Office worker (female)	$850
Factory worker	$1,150
Farm worker	$273

It's a Fact

Business owners were cashing in on the good times. Henry Ford owned the Ford Motor Company. In 1929, Ford reported that his personal income was $14 million. The average American's income that year was $750.

At the same time, people
[s]aw an opportunity to make
[mo]ney by buying **stocks**
[in s]uccessful companies.
[Ow]ning some of a company's
[stoc]k is like owning a part of
[tha]t company. If the value of
[the] stock goes up, people can
[sell] their stock and make a
[pro]fit. In the 1920s, many
[peo]ple borrowed money from
[ban]ks to buy stock.

4. SOLVE THIS!

A man bought stock for
$85 on January 2, 1928. If
he sold the stock one year
later for $420, what was
his profit?

POINT

Reread

How did people make money
by investing in stock?

a stock certificate
from 1923

9

Black Tuesday

For a while, the prices of stocks rose, but then sales began to drop. Businesses cut back production and let many workers go. With workers unemployed, there was even less demand for products. Prices fell even further. And so did the value of stocks. Almost everyone was beginning to lose money.

On Tuesday, October 29, 1929, the value of stocks plunged dramatically. The drop in prices set off a panic. People who owned stocks tried to sell them before the stocks lost even more value. As more and more people tried to sell, stock prices dropped further. By mid-November, the value of stocks had fallen by $30 billion. People began to call October 29th "Black Tuesday."

Crowds gather in New York City's financial area during the stock market crash.

PRIMARY SOURCE

1929   WEATHER—Cloudy · a b c d e f g   TWO CENTS

STOCK VALUES CRASH IN RECORD STAMPEDE

This headline appeared in October 1929. The "record stampede" refers to the rush to sell stocks.

A bank president tries to stop a run on his bank.

Businesses lost so much money that they had to fire workers or close down. People who had borrowed money couldn't repay it. The banks ran out of money and had to shut their doors. By the end of 1930, more than 4 million people were out of work.

It's a Fact

After Black Tuesday, people wanted to withdraw their savings in cash from their banks. Hundreds of people at a time would line up outside a bank to get their money. This was called a "run" on the bank.

Depth of the Depression

By the end of 1932, more than 12 million people—almost a quarter of the labor force—were unemployed. When a job became available, hundreds of people lined up to apply.

For many people there were no jobs at all. They lost their homes, and their families went hungry. Due to lack of money, schools closed and 200,000 teachers lost their jobs.

The stock market crash affected rich and poor alike.

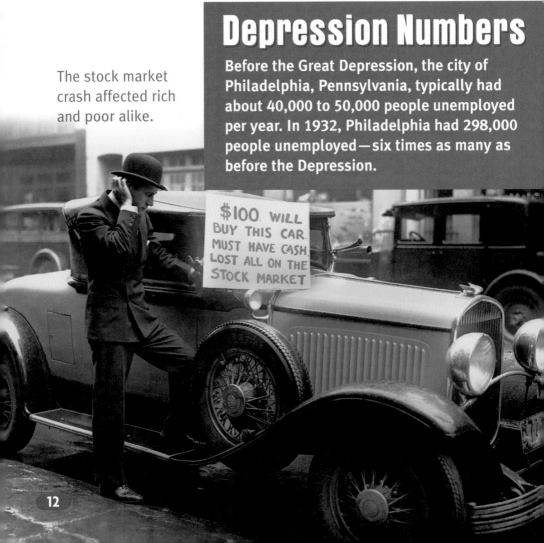

Depression Numbers

Before the Great Depression, the city of Philadelphia, Pennsylvania, typically had about 40,000 to 50,000 people unemployed per year. In 1932, Philadelphia had 298,000 people unemployed—six times as many as before the Depression.

$100. WILL BUY THIS CAR. MUST HAVE CASH. LOST ALL ON THE STOCK MARKET

a shantytown

The Great Depression hit farmers very hard. In 1933, the prices farmers got for their crops were 60 percent lower than they had been in 1929. While millions of people across the country went hungry, farmers couldn't sell the food that they grew. People didn't have the money to pay for it.

The Great Depression was also particularly hard on African Americans. Some employers would fire African American workers to give jobs to white people. The rate of unemployment for African Americans was 60 percent higher than that of white workers.

Hundreds of thousands of Americans lost their homes in 1932. Many of the homeless lived in small shacks on the edges of large cities. Towns of these shacks, or **shantytowns**, had no electricity or running water. The people who lived in them had little food.

A homeless family camps by the side of the road in California during the Great Depression.

The United States had no national **welfare** system at the time of the Great Depression. The U.S. government did not provide relief to the poor in the form of money or food. Many city and state governments did provide relief to the poor. However, with so many people out of work, city and state governments didn't have enough money to provide relief to all who needed it.

5. SOLVE THIS!

a. Suppose a family on relief received $4.23 per week. If the family spent $3.93 a week on food, how much money was left for rent, clothing, electricity, and other expenses?

b. In 1932, the average pair o shoes cost $3.85. Suppose family on relief saved $0.2(per week for five months. Would that be enough money to buy the shoes? Explain your answer.

People who were lucky enough to be employed during the Depression usually didn't make much money. Often workers would take large pay cuts to keep their jobs. It was difficult for people to buy everything they needed to survive.

Depression-Era Prices

Item	Price
Transportation	
Used Ford car	$57.50
Bicycle	$10.95
Clothing	
Cloth coat	$6.98
Shirt	$0.47
Food	
1 dozen eggs	$0.29
1 dozen oranges	$0.27
1 pound of cheese	$0.24
1 pound of pork chops	$0.20
1 quart of milk	$0.10
1 loaf of bread	$0.05

6. SOLVE THIS!

a. Suppose a worker made $432 per year in 1932. If $3/8$ of his income was spent on food, how much money did he spend per year on food?

b. Suppose this worker spent $1/4$ of his income on rent, $3/8$ of his income on food, and $1/8$ of his income on utilities. What part of his income was used to pay other expenses?

People outside an employment agency seek jobs.

The Bonus Army

In 1932, about 20,000 World War I veterans from around the country marched to Washington, D.C. The government had promised to pay these veterans a bonus of $1,000, but not until 1945. The veterans came to Washington to ask for the bonus early. When they arrived, they built a shantytown called the Bonus Army Camp.

The U.S. Congress refused to give the veterans their bonuses. President Herbert Hoover ordered the U.S. army to evict the veterans from their camp. The army used tanks and tear gas to force the veterans out.

By 1932, Herbert Hoover had been president of the United States since the Great Depression began.

President Hoover had done his best to help the country through the hard times. He asked business leaders not to lay off workers or cut wages. He asked state and city governments to help unemployed people. He asked Congress for money to create government projects, which would provide jobs.

President Herbert Hoover

SOLVE THIS!

Use the graph to answer the following questions.

a. Between which of the following years did unemployment increase the most? By how much?

• 1929 and 1930

• 1930 and 1931

• 1931 and 1932

b. In 1932, the number of unemployed was about how many times more than the number of unemployed in 1929?

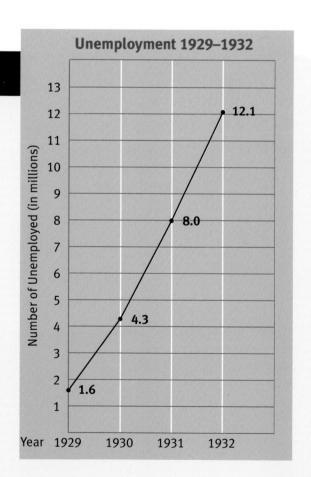

Unemployment 1929–1932

Number of Unemployed (in millions)

1.6 · 4.3 · 8.0 · 12.1

Year 1929 1930 1931 1932

Hoover wanted to help, but he believed that giving money to the poor was a bad idea. He thought this would stop them from trying to help themselves. He also thought that if the U.S. government started a welfare program to give money to the poor, the government would go deeply into debt.

As the Depression got worse, many Americans turned against President Hoover. They thought he wasn't doing enough to help them.

It's a Fact

People made fun of Hoover by naming things after him. These names were called Hooverisms.

Hoover blankets: newspapers under which homeless people slept

Hoover flags: empty pockets turned inside-out

Hoover wagons: broken-down cars pulled by mules

Hoovervilles: shantytowns built of scrap wood and cardboard

a "Hooverville" shantytown in New York City

Franklin D. Roosevelt campaigns to be the president of the United States.

It's a Fact

Franklin D. Roosevelt was born in 1882. When he was 38, he came down with polio, a painful, often deadly disease. It left Roosevelt's legs weak. For the rest of his life, he couldn't walk. Someone once asked him if the Depression had worried him. Roosevelt said, "If you had spent two years in bed trying to wiggle your toe, after that anything would seem easy."

By 1932, people were tired of the Depression, and they were tired of their hard lives. Many of them blamed President Herbert Hoover for the Depression and all their troubles. They were ready for a new president.

Franklin D. Roosevelt ran against Hoover in the presidential election of 1932. With hope that Roosevelt would end the Depression, Americans elected him president.

President Roosevelt's New Deal

The First New Deal

Franklin D. Roosevelt had what he called a "New Deal" for the country. His first act as president was to stop the runs on banks. He ordered all banks closed until Congress could pass laws to help save them. He used this four-day "bank holiday" to convince people to trust the banks. When the banks did open again, bank runs were not a problem.

Roosevelt thought the government should provide jobs and food for the people who needed them. He asked Congress to pass a number of laws, or acts, to create programs that would do this. Many of the programs were known by their initials, such as the AAA and the CCC. People called the new programs "alphabet soup."

PRIMARY SOURCE

This Depression-era cartoon pokes fun at Roosevelt's "alphabet soup" New Deal programs.

One of the New Deal "alphabet soup" programs was the Agricultural Adjustment Act (AAA). This program paid farmers to burn certain crops they had grown. It also paid them to kill thousands of hogs they had raised. Because there were fewer crops and hogs available, their prices went up. Farmers got more income and were able to keep their farms. The AAA wasn't popular with everyone. Some people were angry because crops were burned and animals killed while millions didn't have enough to eat!

They Made a Difference

Every so often, Roosevelt gave a talk on the radio. He called these "fireside chats." It seemed to listeners that he was talking to them while sitting at home beside his fireplace. Millions of Americans listened to these chats. Roosevelt spoke in a friendly way about his ideas and plans for the country. He made people feel that he cared about them. He almost seemed to be a part of their family.

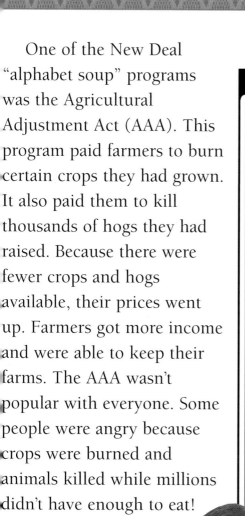

President Franklin Roosevelt delivering one of his "fireside chats"

The National Recovery Administration (NRA) was another "alphabet soup" program. This program asked  business owners to set a minimum wage they would pay workers. The NRA wanted a **minimum wage** of $15 per week for 40 hours of work. The NRA put up posters all over the country. It tried to convince people that this plan was good for the country.

The Public Works Administration (PWA) hired people to build dams, bridges, roads, and public buildings, such as schools and hospitals. Many of these PWA projects are still around today. The Grand Coulee Dam on the Columbia River in the state of Washington is one.

The Grand Coulee Dam was a Public Works Administration project.

The Civil Works Administration (CWA) hired about 4 million people. CWA workers built 40,000 schools, 469 airports, and 255,000 miles of streets and roads.

The Civilian Conservation Corps (CCC) provided work for thousands of men between the ages of 17 and 27. The men were fed and housed in work camps. In return, they cleared land and planted 2 billion trees in national parks and forests and on other government land. They also fought fires and cleaned reservoirs.

The Tennessee Valley Authority (TVA) built dams. These dams were used to generate electricity for poor communities in the South. The TVA also started programs in **soil conservation**. Its programs taught people how to farm without damaging the land.

8. SOLVE THIS!

Suppose a Civilian Conservation Corps worker planted trees in rows on a square plot of land. That plot was 70 yards long on each side (about one acre in area). He planted the first tree in one of the corners. He then planted the rest of the trees seven yards apart in rows. How many trees could he fit on the plot of land?

POINT

Make Connections

Roosevelt's public works programs built roads, schools, and other projects all over the country. Are any of them in your community? A librarian in your school media center or a local library could help you find out.

President Roosevelt was not always sure which of his New Deal "alphabet soup" programs would work and which ones wouldn't. The programs did not provide permanent jobs. But they did help people survive the most difficult years of the Great Depression.

These Civilian Conservation Corps workers are preparing two-year-old fir trees for transplanting.

9. SOLVE THIS!

In 1935, the Civilian Conservation Corps employed 500,000 men and paid them $30 per month. Most of them lived in camps and sent their money home. If, during one of those months, all the CCC workers had sent all of their money home, what would have been the total sent home in that one month?

The Dust Bowl

While things were improving for many people because of the New Deal, parts of the Great Plains were facing an additional crisis. In 1933, parts of the Great Plains were suffering from a long drought. There had been almost no rain for two years! High winds carried dry topsoil into the air. The soil became part of huge dust storms that buried farms and killed crops. The area became known as the Dust Bowl.

Thousands of farmers gave up. They packed their few remaining belongings and walked or drove to California. Many people living in cities in the Dust Bowl states also left their homes. In the 1930s, some 350,000 people took to the roads. People often called

Most Okies lived in their trucks as they made their way to California.

these migrants "Okies," because so many came from Oklahoma. In California, many migrants worked as fruit-pickers and lived in shacks, barely able to feed their families.

The Second New Deal

By 1935, Roosevelt saw that more programs were needed to help the country. Things were better, but millions of Americans were still without work. He asked Congress to pass laws to create new programs. These programs are sometimes called the "Second New Deal."

The Works Progress Administration (WPA) created more jobs, including jobs for people in the arts. Photographers, painters, writers, actors, and musicians worked on public projects. These jobs paid up to $94.90 a month. The average wage was about $50 a month.

The Social Security Act helped people survive when they were out of work. As a result of this act, the government took a percentage of a worker's income and set it aside in a savings account. Then, if the worker lost a job or retired, he or she would receive monthly payments from this account.

A WPA artist works on a mural.

26

Despite the NRA's efforts to encourage a minimum wage, many employers were still paying their employees very low wages. But the Fair Labor Standards Act of 1938 changed that by setting a minimum wage of 25 cents an hour. This law also made it illegal to force anyone to work more than 44 hours a week.

Roosevelt's programs helped somewhat. Then in 1941, the United States entered World War II. American factories that built planes, weapons, and other things for the war needed a lot of workers. Jobs became much more plentiful, and the economy greatly improved. As World War II blazed, the Great Depression faded away.

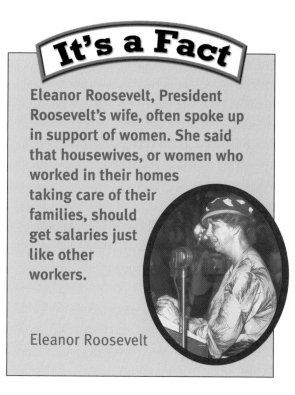

It's a Fact

Eleanor Roosevelt, President Roosevelt's wife, often spoke up in support of women. She said that housewives, or women who worked in their homes taking care of their families, should get salaries just like other workers.

Eleanor Roosevelt

10. SOLVE THIS!

a. Suppose a woman worked in her home for 15 hours a day. If she were paid for that work at $0.25 per hour and worked 6 days a week, how much would she have made in a week?

b. If that same woman spent 1/5 of her weekly wages on food, how much would she spend on food in one week?

Conclusion

The Great Depression caused great hardships for millions of Americans. At its height, 27 percent of the workforce was unemployed. People who were working often took big cuts in pay to keep their jobs.

Use the graph to answer the following questions.

a. For the years shown, which year had the highest number of unemployed people?

b. Describe the trend in unemployment from 1933 to 1941.

c. Which year showed the third lowest number of unemployed people?

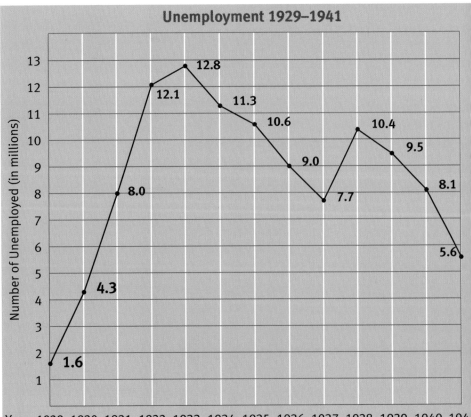

Unemployment 1929–1941

Number of Unemployed (in millions)

1.6 · 4.3 · 8.0 · 12.1 · 12.8 · 11.3 · 10.6 · 9.0 · 7.7 · 10.4 · 9.5 · 8.1 · 5.6

Year 1929 1930 1931 1932 1933 1934 1935 1936 1937 1938 1939 1940 194

President Franklin D. Roosevelt started many programs to help pull the country out of the Great Depression. But it did not end completely until the United States entered World War II.

Before the Depression, government leaders had done little to help when the U.S. economy slumped. They had assumed that the problems would fix themselves. The Great Depression changed this. It forced the government to take action.

Because of the Depression, the government took on a stronger role in keeping the economy stable. It created better "safety nets" to protect people from economic problems. After the Great Depression, people knew that the government would give them more financial protection than it had before.

The United States has had times of economic trouble since the Great Depression. But none has been as serious as that crisis was. Hopefully, such a crisis will never happen again.

During the Great Depression, many people stood in long lines to get free food, such as a bowl of soup. This monument is a memorial to those times.

SOLVE THIS!
Answers

1. Page 3
a. 1930
b. 1930–1933; 19%
c. 56 million

2. Page 5
a. 23 million
b. 16 million

3. Page 8
a. $25
b. $5.25

4. Page 9
$335

5. Page 14
a. $0.30
b. yes;
5 months = 20 weeks;
$0.20 X 20 = $4.00

6. Page 15
a. $162
b. 1/4

7. Page 17
a. 1931 and 1932;
4.1 million
b. about 8 times more

8. Page 23
121

9. Page 24
$15,000,000

10. Page 27
a. $22.50 per week
b. $4.50

11. Page 28
a. 1933
b. Unemployment fell
steadily from 1933
through 1937, rose in
1938, then fell steadily
again from 1938 through
1941.
c. 1941

Glossary

credit   (KREH-diht) a system of buying something without paying all at once, and instead, paying a certain amount each week or month (page 6)

depression   (dih-PREH-shuhn) a time when a country's economy is doing badly; products do not sell, and people have trouble finding jobs (page 2)

minimum wage   (MIH-nih-muhm WAYJ) the lowest wage a business can legally pay a worker (page 22)

prosperity   (PRAH-sper-ih-tee) an economic time of well-being (page 4)

shantytown   (SHAN-tee-town) a town of shacks; the Bonus Army camp was a shantytown (page 13)

soil conservation   (SOYL kahn-ser-VAY-shuhn) a way of farming that also ensures the soil will be useful for a longer period of time (page 23)

stock   (STAHK) a piece of a company that a person can buy, also known as shares (page 9)

unemployed   (uhn-ehm-PLOYD) out of work and unable to find a job (page 2)

veteran   (VEHT-er-ihn) a person who has served in the armed forces (page 16)

welfare   (WEHL-fayr) a government system set up to help people when they are unemployed, homeless, hungry, or poor (page 14)

Index